Holonym

a collection of poems by

Trish Lindsey Jaggers

Finishing Line Press
Georgetown, Kentucky

Holonym

Wage words not war. Trish Lindsey Jaggers, 9/11/2001

Copyright © 2016 by Trish Lindsey Jaggers
ISBN 978-1-944899-15-8 First Edition
All rights reserved under International and Pan-American Copyright Conventions. No part of this book may be reproduced in any manner whatsoever without written permission from the publisher, except in the case of brief quotations embodied in critical articles and reviews.

ACKNOWLEDGMENTS

Grateful acknowledgment is extended to the editors of the following journals in which these poems, sometimes in different versions, first appeared:

On the Night They Took Your Life	*New Millennium Writings* (winner)
Holonym	*The Louisville Review*
On Finding Black Judgement	*New Southerner* (finalist)
Murmuring of Stones	*Paperfields Press Poet of the Month*
The Very Last Phone Booth	*Paperfields Press Poet of the Month*
Jaybirds Feeding on Robins	*Paperfields Press Poet of the Month*
	Goodreads Poetry Contest (winner)
To Away	*The Round Table* (award winner)
Penknife	*Poetry Midwest*
While I Wait	*Briar Cliff Review*
After Reading the Gold Cell	*The Round Table*
Daylight Savings Time	*Red Rock Review*
Petal	*The Louisville Review*
Scottie	*Literary Mama*
The Moon Can See the Light of Day	*New Southerner* (finalist)

Many of the poems in this collection have been semifinalists, finalists, and honorable mentions in several prestigious contests. While not all were published, I'm grateful for the honors.

Thank you: to Jennie Brown, my first mentor, for the delightful hours of coffee and the flight of wise, black-winged words in the margins; for tireless ears of my revisions, my workshop friends/colleagues: Danny Shepherd, Tim Brotherton, Diana McQuady, Lou-Ann Crouther, and Carole Baum; Mary Ellen Miller, a great mentor and friend; and especially for my family: my late father, the "like-a poet" who taught me metaphor; my late mother and her perfect shade of blue; son-in-law Bryan for technically keeping my words alive (more than once); eagle-eyed Scott, my son, who misses nothing; daughter Bridgette, my number one fan, with an ear for the music (and the occasional dull thud) of words; and husband Kelly, for 35 years of letting me sleep late so I could finish my dreams.

Editor: Christen Kincaid
Cover Art: Trish Lindsey Jaggers
Author Photo: Bridgette Dawn Jaggers
Cover Design: Bryan Dennison

Printed in the USA on acid-free paper.
Order online: www.finishinglinepress.com
also available on amazon.com

Author inquiries and mail orders:
Finishing Line Press
P. O. Box 1626
Georgetown, Kentucky 40324
U. S. A.

Table of Contents

While I Wait 1

Vestiges 3

On Finding *Black Judgement*..4

Ars Longa, Vita Brevis 6

Murmuring of Stones..7

It's Getting Late Earlier Now..9

On the Night They Took Your Life.............................11

Scottie..13

Neighbors 16

Holonym..17

Jaybirds Feeding on Robins..18

Daylight Savings Time..21

Observations of an Autumnal Equinox......................24

Penknife 25

The Moon Can See the Light of Day.........................26

Shade...28

After Reading the Gold Cell.......................................30

Petal...31

Skydive 32

The Very Last Phone Booth 33

To the Fountain Pen in the Clearance Box at the
    Antique Store 35

To Away 36

To the Best Times of My Life 37

While I Wait

for the pot to fill—
strong coffee takes longer to drip—
and open the quiet door
a bit wider, I let the answering machine
silence an old friend
because she reminds me
how cappuccino tastes
outside the moments spent in sage
green coffee shops, our spines
pressed into cherry
slats of mismatched chairs,
while restless feet work the rungs
loose from the legs,
as she tells me
there's so much more than this
to live for—
while I wince-swallow
blistered foam, try
to figure out why I asked
for cappuccino
and not jamocha
or espresso,
and why I don't
order one anyway,
and I pretend to read
her flight itinerary, follow a trail
of straightened coffee spoons
dropped on mahogany hard-wood
floors, while footsteps carry in
pastel dust from poems
chalked on the sidewalk,

and bouquets of white napkin roses
bloom on twisted strawpaper stems
inside empty, chipped ceramic mugs
still sticky with words.

Vestiges

Our backs together, the sun and I lean
into the staple-studded power pole
cornering the outskirts of town.
Rain-wrinkled words on flyers—
"Free High School Musical,"
a collie named Larry
lost last year. "Have You Seen Me?"
Eyes are familiar mirrors.
Do missing children ever see
their own posters? Iced pictures melting in the snow
outside the coffee shop. Cappuccino rings.
Sticky tables. Pennies in a tip jar. What if this is all
the flash we get before we die? Eight trilled notes,
the sparrow wise in her song.
Last night I dreamed
I was on a flight to London, but I woke
in a cheap hotel, my fingers bare. I had to cut the rings
from my mother's dead hand. Out here, no one lives
that close to anyone anymore.

On Finding *Black Judgement*
*for Nikki Giovanni**

By the front entrance of the small county
library, the "withdrawn" books. This one
a dime. Already on its way out.
In the beginning was the word
And the word was
Death
"Discard" stamped across
her left cheek, the black and white
photograph sneaked inside the back cover,
like it had to. Like it had to. Nikki G's revolution

"Withdrawn," shut tight inside
the faded brown-shaded covers. A rebel
flag drawn over the back window of a white
pickup truck parked across two spaces outside
the library, like it was stamped there. Like it had to.
The flag's reds arrowing in, like blood. Like anemia.

Nineteen years later, near the eve of Juneteenth.
Nine names withdrawn,
stamped out of the registry
in the South Carolina church
one pale Trojan horse was welcomed into.
There had to be one.

Please, say their names, they say.
Peace be still, Nikki says.
Only the torch can show the way

As kids, we drew in the night air
with sparklers, made circles and crosses of fire,
the dark streaked red. The rings and X's lingered
like a stain, until we could see them

with our eyes closed, see them insist on staying
alive. *Peace be still*

I won't say his name. But it is many. It is death.

Bibles drawn in front of him, the table spread
with words. I*n the beginning was the deed*
And the deed was death
and her words sold for a dime.

Words make dying sound easy.

He is forgiven.
Already. They pray for him, Peace be still
The X drawn over a red-stained heritage
he protects as though someone can take it from him,
as though it could ever be lost, even on purpose.

Inside his red and white cover he stamps
Withdrawn, Withdrawn, Withdrawn
Withdrawn, Withdrawn, Withdrawn
Withdrawn, Withdrawn, Withdrawn.

Then he drives away. He simply drives away.

Say their names for Nikki G. Please, say their names.
The rumblings of this peace must be stilled
be stilled be still.

---

*Italicized lines are from Giovanni's "The Great Pax White" as
it appeared in *Black Judgement*, 1971

Ars Longa, Vita Brevis
to Archibald MacLeish

Not true, MacLeish.
Bird words punctuate the still, leave, then arrive,
commas and dashes on oak limbs.

A poem must speak; its breath
just lift the lid of the inner eye, then cool
the drops gathered there.

Move, as a flower unspins, flings
yellow dust on dark legs and white wings.
Stir the air, petal by petal.

Stay, staccato notes dropped
branch by branch,
from tree to moonlit tree.

Stay, a birthmark on the mind. Not a stain.
But almost.

Eclipse, spread fingers between sight and sun;
world of blood blocked by skin.

Laugh, stretch inside the doorway, take up space.

Silence, no. There's still the mortar. And tick
of thirst. And groans from babies' moms.

Love, love us to death. Leaning grasses, switched
by briars. Dark slung across the sea.
Make us want to be.

Honest. Willing to lie for the sake of truth. And die.
That means, too.

Murmuring of Stones

I collect the earth,
gather it loosely in bags;
rocks, the diary of stones'

years, earth-baked ridges,
stratified chips and gravel,
secrets pressed silent.

Even as a child, I wanted the earth
to read its pages, let loose its layers,
tattle in my bag, the clicking of tongues

like mothers telling children to behave,
like cocking hammers of guns,
like people turning to dust, dust to stone,

their cold bones warming
in my hand, my hand cooling
around them, their fossils indenting

my palm; rivers of lifelines
etched deeper than skin,
deeper than bone;

beneath the cracking crust, red ages beat
the drums of clubs, of arrows, of daggers;
the lead, the shrapnel, glint in dying

light, earth folding in,
walls of stone
coming undone;

those who went
are coming home, on this gravel road;
quartz—sun-winking, begging

for my hand, my bag. There's room.
I choose stones because I can't leave them,
because they are

different from each other,
even those clawed from the face
of one mountain; stones can't lie

still for long, their stories unchanged,
the way moss is green without sun,
yet changing, the way a stone

eddies the rush of river,
the way stones crush each other,
mix and press new stones, bagsful

of rocks and sand, finite and infinite
roads and footpaths, disappearing, stolen,
a grit at a time.

As we leave the river and take the gravel
path back to the car, my body a comma
against my bag's weight,

you open the driver's door for me, help me
unhook the bag from its dent in my shoulder, ask
"What do you have in there—rocks?"

and I throw back my head and laugh

It's Getting Late Earlier Now
to Bridgette, for saying that when you were five

They started early,
before the evening sun tie-dyed the sky.
I lean against the oak and watch.
The air crisps, crackles,
explodes—points trailing color—
rainbows melt.

The air greys, hangs; tang of gunpowder
burns my nose, my tongue.
A sliver of peace slices the night
of July fireworks. Dark seems darker,
too still,
like the silence after a gunshot.

An insect grabs my arm,
and I slap what I can't see.

Yellow/green flashes, once, twice,
disappears in the grass.
How could I have known
that a firefly would choose me,
mistake my warmth?

Does it get like that?
Does it get that easy to kill?
Another thunder.

I close my eyes, try to imagine
the Iraq war, any war,
if the rumbles and cracks,
the three-beat rhythms of precision,

sound like this,
if I could close my eyes
every night to that, how early
the night would come,
how long it would last.
Would I hear the children,
the women, dying?

A bottle rocket screams
too close to home, and suddenly,
I almost know.

On the Night They Took Your Life

There was a ring around the moon,
and I went looking for you, outside, when the stale air inside
grew too easy, too still, and my knitting stomach
slipped its stitches.

There you were, you were,
between the old April cracks thawed
through the ground, and the stars
we'd shared since you left me, left me, left

my body. I said, "What's the matter, baby?"
and I wanted you back,
a baby, my baby—
fastened to my breast,

your breath, my life,
white drops pearled around your tiny mouth—
just so you'd believe me once again
when I say, "The world is your Milky Way."

You were there, beneath the sugar maples,
their syrups drumming against thin wood; you
cast no shadow in their shade, the moon a ring
of light at your feet.

You said, "I just need to see the earth
from the sky," and I knew
the war had sliced the moon
from your sky, shot

all the light from your stars. You were glad
to be home, on this farm, on this hill,
where the circles of night sky
meet the torn edges of land.

You said, "There's a ring
around the moon," and we sat together
beneath the ring. The moon waxed colder
behind a hush of haze, threw unsteady light

on your unreadable face. I drew you close,
felt your baby ring, safe on its silver chain,
tight against my throat, said, "Talk to me,
tell me everything. Let it go."

I need to share the air, warm
as the edge of autumn—a slow-turning season,
when the pulse slows, green to yellow, to red—slow
as the syrup slipping over the edge

of your plate this morning, when I called your name,
knew from the sound of your empty bed
that the shrapnel of broken stars cut you
from me, from me, from me

Scottie

Your daddy cried first
with the sound pain makes—
when it's wrapped up tight, tight
as empty, and it still leaks out
in gasps and wheezes,
with a little choking.
And the shaking.

I sat on your bed, knew
you would be back
in a few minutes,
maybe a day—for good measure—
but, nonetheless, you'd come crawling
back, say, "Oops! I forgot something,"
something like "I love you, and I want to stay
here until I have to leave, until
you push me out. Sorry Daddy,
for making you cry."

Your daddy and I breathed
the last scent of you
as we walked through your bedroom,
fingered spaces, spaces
where this used to sit, and that sat
for so long. I turned my back
when he pulled out a drawer.
I didn't want to see
the bottom, all four
corners, neatly bare.

Your daddy played with your toys—toys
you left—folded each piece
of trash before he threw it away.

Your daddy's shoulders curved,
bowed like a lily in a vase
after the water drops below
the descending axis of life. Life—
odd how it descends and not ascends;
we grow up not down,
and others droop;
their shoulders curve.

You wanted to be called "Scott,"
and we shrank
three or four inches,
looked up to you.
I said, "Take off those shoes right now."
You said, "I'm not
wearing any."

We have unfinished
business to take care of.
We need to go fishing one more time,
stand on the rocks
at the water's edge and pick mud
out of our fingernails,
worms off our hands,
say nothing,
catch nothing,
call it a day—
a good day—
because the shade was cool
and the water as still
as your room now.

Holonym

There is a shade of white
the hospital pillowcase
turns, after the head
leaves it, after the heat
leaves the imprint,
sheets and towels pushed away
like bathwater foam;
and the smell grows, the shampoo,
the thin sliver of soap dried to the bottom
of the plastic washtub, dead
bubbles dusting its sides;
and the straw-tip bows lower
in the plastic glass as sweat hesitates,
then slips over fingerprints;
wisps of white and almost white
curled into the thin teeth
of the complimentary comb.
And the blinds are slightly open,
like his eyes were
before I closed them,
light coming through in stripes,
slow-crossing the room
like a white tiger.

Jaybirds Feeding on Robins

They are at it again. Momma
robin tears through the trees to save
what's left of her babies. One lies
twitching on the ground, its eye socket
emptied by a jay. I can't bury it
until it's dead, and I can't kill it,
so I sit by it
beneath the screaming nest in the sugar maple
as rain drops sizzle through hot leaves.

It's June, and it's supposed to be like this,
daylong heat frying up evening
thunderstorms. In the west, new cumulonimbus
stretch their gargoyle heads, growl long and low.
If it were dark, I could see lightning
ricochet from cloud to cloud. Thunderheads,
Daddy called them.

Four summers ago, a palm reader
told me that a man I love
is slipping away,
a dandelion letting go of its seed,
the seed grasping the stalk in the west wind.

Daddy was afraid of leaving
for anywhere not close to home.
He always wanted to swim
in the ocean, but I went first,
came back thanking him
for my life. Last time I dragged myself home
from the white edges of Georgia's coast,
past the palm-reader's house,

past the lily-pad-covered swamps,
past tired cattails fuzzing out seeds,
he'd bought a van, "Next year,
we all can go, and you can drive."

The reader said that I pass many
but travel alone because
I'm afraid of loss, of being left.
I closed my hand to this fool before she took
any more of my money
or my palm.

The twitching stops. Rain runs
down my face, tugs free of my chin.
"All rain runs to the ocean," he'd said.

The earth is dry
beneath the bird. I triangle-fold it
into one of his old hankies,
lift a corner just before the earth goes in.
I want to be sure.

The wedge of its beak is cold,
arrowed like the sharks' teeth
I found on Cumberland Island.
Above me, in a high fork
of the sugar maple he planted
twenty-six years ago,
the screaming has stopped.

He'll be dead four years this August.
I sold the van. He'd parked it
in the sugar maple's shadow,
the grass pale and stiff when I moved it.
Today, I leave for Georgia.

In the west, the thunderheads shake
out their dark fur; the wind rakes
rain and leaves from the trees;
years of roots and worms and earth
steam from the ground. I pat it down, make a cross
with rocks like we did when I was four.
"Why do jays do that?" I'd asked.
"It's their nature," he'd said.

I stand, drag my muddy hands across my jeans.
I taste salt
in the back of my throat.
If I hurry, the storm will be behind me as I drive.

Daylight Savings Time

This is one of those days
when everyone left me,
one of those
obtuse days
when the wind won't stop
pulling at my feet
and pushing at my hair
until I bend.
I can't find the smooth
side of friction,
but I can smell it;
one of those days
when friction leaves
a tang of burn,
a hint of blue
denim, the rub of rough
sandpaper inside out,
and I acquiesce,
split like daisy petals,
lie flat and spread
my lily-white-self
for people to walk past,
give their eyes
a place to close for a second.

This is one of those days
when grass grows in clumps,
kills the mower
and scatters cut green petals
of onion, clover, and sour doc
downwind, past the Brownsville Post Office
and the CeeBee Food Store,

past True Value Hardware
and Lindsey's Barber Shop,
past the Sun Valley Feed Mill
and the Edmonson County Library,
past the Apothecary
and Patton's Funeral Home,
past Madison's Flower Bouquet
and sticks to the face of a man
eating an Eskimo Pie on a picnic table
outside Birdie's Ice Cream shop;

one of those days
my head fills with angles
through all those open places
where slanted stuff can fit.
My ears are straws
that my brain drinks through
and so are my fingers and tongue.
One of those days
when I'd like to swim
in the rain, but my ears might fill
with drizzle and trees
and I would drown;

one of those days
when everyone left me,
and I go down to the river,
stand there
without a voice,
be one continuous line,
a ninety-degree angle
spread flat,

and drink river language,
the language
of water and tree-speak;

one of those days,
one of those angles
that goes beyond right,
one of those crooked
triangular days
when I'm glad they left me
alone because I can't hear
what with all that noise anyway,

one of those scalene days
when a hundred and fifty proof
and a drop of raspberry tint
are all the glass can hold;
one of those days
friction creates,
and I try to cool my lips,
but the ice cracks
free of itself and floats
above the surface.
And I just can't touch numb.

Observations of an Autumnal Equinox

Inside,
it's one a.m.; outside,
a robin sings from its perch
in the moon's crooked dark.

I watch a star flicker,
until it moves
and the slow, sinking thunder
of jet engine follows it.

On the other side of the hill,
not one of Vincent's hunting dogs
is barking tonight. For a change,
I miss this.

The lamp in my upstairs window
spreads the pale butter of light
over the pulse of dusty wings
beating against the glass.

Ahead of me, circles of anthills
spot my gravel drive,
dark scabs on the long dusty leg
curved over the hill.

I lean against what lightning left
of the oak tree. Summer's bewitched
leaves gather and rise
in a whispering pile around it.

A cricket jumps against my leg
as it tries to get somewhere,
and I move
out of its way.

Penknife

Inside the antique store,
within the locked glass
case, beside the reading
glasses that slipped midway
down a white plastic nose,
behind the ivory-handled letter
opener—the one with the greened-out
brass knife, the kind that can't be sharpened—
that lies across an uncut seal—
one of those with a monogram
writhing and twisting inside its circle
like red-worm wigglers
left to sun in the muddy bottom
of a rusted Eight-O-Clock can,
at three o'clock, Solar Noon,
when the fish stop biting at the foaming mouth
of Bear Creek—
the wax-slicked surface
that rises and falls like river trash
almost hid the old penknife—
nearly closed,
as the lips of a dying mussel—
a pencil shaving curled into its crevice
as though a tongue wanted to speak sharpened words
but decided against it.

The Moon Can See the Light of Day

It is easy to believe the earth stands still,
that each night the little dipper hangs from a different nail,
that the moon follows the lamp of sun as it counts its till
from the day's tips and tabs and yesterday's unopened mail.

And each night, the little dipper hangs from a different nail
driven deep into the dark ceiling
above yesterday's tips and tabs and weeks of unopened mail.
Beneath the turning sky, the whippoorwill bleeds its song,

nails the stain deep into the dark ceiling.
The mockingbird, too, rehearses its song at midnight.
Hidden by the silent turning sky, the whippoorwill's vein of song,
a quatrain followed by a couplet.

At midnight, the mockingbird practices its song,
a ballad of other birds' old rhymes and repetitions—
same
old
same
old
brand
new
tally, four-lines and a cross, and the sky turns on.

Small speckled eggs birth more old rhymes.
The morning sweats into arousal,
ticking off time, four lines and a cross.
A feather swims across the streaming song of birds.

The sweaty morning writhes as the moon pulls away
from sassafras leaves dipped in dew.
A feather seeks the breath of song, of day.
The sunflower lifts her head from sleep

beneath sassafras leaves dipped in dew.
I sit outside with coffee and mending.
The sunflower lifts her heavy head.
Across the bur-cut field, hay rolls strain to stay.

I slow-sip the brine of coffee, shirt bunched, button in hand;
the thread splays before the needle's eye.
Over the dry crackling grass, the hay rolls lean.
The sun turns everything morning, a crayon of sky.

The thread splays before the needle's eye.
clouds gather, mate, and separate,
A melted box of crayons—sun, sky.
My hand shakes behind the thread.

Clouds gather, mate, and separate.
The rain lifts her skirt as she steps over our hill.
Behind the needle's narrowed eye, my hand shakes.
It is easy to believe the earth stands still.

Shade

I don't like blue
because Momma filled
our rooms with it, carried it
all over the house
like footprints, and Daddy helped her
pick it out of other stray
colors that I wanted
to bring home. He told her which blues
belonged and which ones
cost too much. She slipped
her own shade of blue
covers around the broken
edges of beds, window cracks,
and hard pillows, bought blue
soap, blue towels, and blue hairbrushes
to pull the blue-grey
from her blue-black hair,
blue toilet paper and tissues,
and I made torn roses
and carnations that looked
almost real. She sought blue
on sale—blue salt
and pepper shakers, blue sleep-
wear, blue panties, and blue glass
ashtrays she never used
because they showed grey
dust, blue coats, blue trash
bags to put over her navy blue clothes.
She wore blood-red lipstick and scarlet
nail polish. She wanted her coffin
to be blue—and also her dress—

when she died to show off the red
rose she wanted to hold.
I fell in love with purple
while I was still too young to know
purple is blue
with just one drop
of red.

After Reading The Gold Cell
to Sharon Olds

You take me into the study, walls where your family
portraits were, now only squares and rectangles,
afterimages of frames burned in paint.
I take your book off the shelf
again, flit its pages beneath my nose.

I know this smell, the raw of sex waiting,
the metallic scent that keys leave
on my hand if I linger too long
at the lock.

I want to close the book,
skitter from the room, the way a bird leaves
the safe height of her tree,
after some perceived threat
rattles the ground beneath her,
instead of staying still,
staying alive.

Petal

When it is perfect,
it is alive, not still;
this fist of rose bud
unfurls its red self
like the spider,
frightened into a ball,
untucks her eight legs
in the near-bottom
of a steel sink
as the water that almost
caught her
slinks toward the drain,
and she crawls back,
works all night, crisscrossing
that drain; her red body
dripping, legs busy
grasping and pulling
thread from somewhere deep
inside her, not afraid
of death, but the letting
go

Skydive

And this time, without a parachute.
I will unfold my unmailed letter
from its yellowed envelope, lean into the blue
bed, and fall, elbows first, into the seamless
comforter of cloud.

Sure, I know, the ground waits below,
hidden by a crazy, crazy quilt,
its patches crooked and tattered,
the twisted, knotted threads of its flags
flapping like sheets on the line,
but it waits just the same for everyone,
and most won't ever know
how a seed blown free feels
before planting.

The Very Last Phone Booth

bare bulb the spiders would not touch. what is outside is nothing. what is inside is everywhere. time cobbed in corners. the people I said I'd call, the places I promised I would go, the acres my feet itched to touch. I cheated my skin, my soles. prisoners of my will nots. my body of dust held still by webs.

crack open the door. let the light out. the glass is too smudged to bleed it. each fiber in my head a live wire. one electrical pulse, you know, like in an old phone—not enough to kill me, but if we were submerged together I would want to divorce that water.

light thickens the mahogany syrup of dark. the seat whitewashed with twisted tissues. I'm sorrys and I love yous and will you ever come homes, and yesses and oh yesses, stretched and fileted as grandma's crocheted lace on the chair arm. light lets loose from the lamp, and what is seen cannot disappear again.

one of these days, all new will be over, too, and what remains, others will pick through, a rummage sale of sorts. snap pictures and send to friends. "look at this old thing I found. if only it could talk." perhaps, it would not say a word, and the world would be better off because of it.

how many nights did the drunk sleep here? cigarettes burned to the filter. ashes don't die, you know. they are dead already. we think. a greying anachronism still pink and hot beneath the whiskey. call 911! the world is on fire, everywhere, and the water dried up. here and there, over there, that is all that's left. doesn't look so bad, now, outside the light, does it?

at least, the night takes up no space. there'll always be dark waiting outside of things, underneath things, behind things, inside the cushion that sleep curls up on when the wind outside is just too damned cold. and the iced words left, when the spare change ran out, numb the tongue—still stuck fast to the arctic metal of the phone booth's door—and evaporate like breath on its cracked glass.

To the Fountain Pen in the Clearance Box at the Antique Store

You there, the scratched one—gold faded
from your cap like an old glass Christmas ball
fallen between rafters in the attic. Your body,
not quite straight, not quite bent,
like you almost melted once, like just in time,
someone took you out of the fire,
or took the heat away, your body now hunkered
against the permanence of new cold.
There's a stain of black at your edge,
once fed by a vein deep in your body.
Your cartridge is gone and, with it, your ink,

but maybe not. Maybe, the ink sleeps somewhere
on crisp sheets bundled by strings,
like Emily Dickinson's poetry,
packed away like rations in wartime,
a pantry of words to chew or choke
on. What if I buy you? Would you mind
my fumbling with your head,
your body, forcing myself
to fit the curve of you?
Would you stand if I find I cannot
use you, stand,
your back curved like a picked flower
wilting in my vase of other dried-up pens?

To Away

All leaving things come
to you though they must leave
in order to reach you
the yellow squat house on the corner
came to you
during the tornado
the white wicker rocker
and the old man with the grey eyes
they say he went
to your locked rooms too
dry snow fog
all appear in the vanishing point
of your arms
the wind
and breath
when it has its way
last fall's leaves and dandelion seeds
shadows and mountain streams
left socks and memory
all kneel at your altar
I've looked for you for years
always on the disappearing trail
of something that found you
first

To the Best Times of My Life

To talk to
or even look at you
I find I must turn back
the leaves of you
dog-eared moments

how could I not see you then
why didn't I realize you were
special, real, something
that I could not redo
nor want to
undo

the spines of your days line up
crooked on the shelves
burgundy seconds
clasped air in my hand
and I feel your tender turning
returning
and never coming back
again

Trish Lindsey Jaggers was born in Louisville, Kentucky, adopted at age six months, and transplanted as a preteen into Southcentral Kentucky. She never looked back. She feels, intensely, the pain of the world. War, discrimination, and poverty form much of the serrated edge of her writing "blade."

She is an award-winning Kentucky poet, educator, feminist, amateur photographer, vintage/antique collector, as well as wife, mother of two, and grandmother She has published in numerous literary magazines, journals, books, and anthologies. She earned a BA in English at Western Kentucky University and an MFA in creative writing from Spalding University.

She is an assistant professor of English at Western Kentucky University. She makes her home on a small farm in Chalybeate, Kentucky, where she divides her time among the quiet spaces nature so abundantly offers, her family, collecting, travel, teaching, and of course, writing. As with the perfect poem, piece of prose, photograph, and antique, she finds the elusive most intriguing and worthy of the time spent in search of it.

Her poems have appeared (or are upcoming) in *New Millennium Writings* (winner of the NMW Poetry Award #26); *New Southerner Literary Edition* (finalist in the New Southerner Literary Prizes); *The Briar Cliff Review; The Louisville Review; New Southerner; Round Table; Matter 11: The Woods; So to Speak; The Red Rock Review; Clackamas Literary Review; Oh Sister, My Sister: An Anthology on Sisterhood; The Creative Arc: Anthology of Writing on Writing; Motif: Writing by Ear; Coming of Age: A Treasury of Poems; The Heartland Review; The Tobacco Anthology*, and other journals, books, and anthologies.

In addition to winning the *New Millennium Writings* Poetry Award #26, she's won the "Night Rider Award" (Round Table), placed second in the Carnegie Center's "Next Great Writer Award," placed first in the May 2009 Goodreads Poetry Contest, was a finalist for the Joy Bale Boone Poetry Prize, was a finalist in the *New Southerner* Literary Contest (twice), and placed or was an honorable mention in several other awards, slams, and contests.

www.ingramcontent.com/pod-product-compliance
Lightning Source LLC
Chambersburg PA
CBHW060223050426
42446CB00013B/3149